This Candlewick book
belongs to:

_____

_____

In memory of my mum,
who taught me to sew
C. B.

To all the babies of my
family and friends
L. G.

Text copyright © 2015 by Chris Butterworth
Illustrations copyright © 2015 by Lucia Gaggiotti

First U.S. paperback edition 2017

Library of Congress Catalog Card Number 2014951787
ISBN 978-0-7636-7750-3 (hardcover)
ISBN 978-0-7636-9518-7 (paperback)

17 18 19 20 21 22 TWP 10 9 8 7 6 5 4 3 2 1

Printed in Johor Bahru, Malaysia

This book was typeset in VAG Rounded.
The illustrations were done in mixed media.

Candlewick Press
99 Dover Street
Somerville, Massachusetts 02144

visit us at www.candlewick.com

Chris Butterworth

WHERE DID MY CLOTHES COME FROM?

EXPLORING THE EVERYDAY

illustrated by **Lucia Gaggiotti**

CANDLEWICK PRESS

WOULDN'T it be great if you could wear your favorite clothes ALL the time?

But you need different clothes for different weather and for doing different things.

You need warm clothes for cold days, cool clothes for hot days, and clothes to keep you dry in the rain.

You need fancy clothes and clothes to get messy in.

But what are your clothes made of?

And where did they come from?

WHAT ARE YOUR JEANS MADE OF?

Your jeans are made of cotton, and cotton grows on bushes!

A cotton seed needs lots of sun and water to grow into a bush.

It takes about ten weeks for a flower to bloom. After the flower dies, a seedpod called a cotton boll swells and ripens.

fibers

In a few more weeks, the boll splits open and soft, snowy-white cotton fibers puff out.

The bolls are picked (by hand or by machine).

Then a machine called a gin gets rid of the seeds tangled in the cotton fibers.

The cleaned cotton is put into bales and taken to a spinning mill.

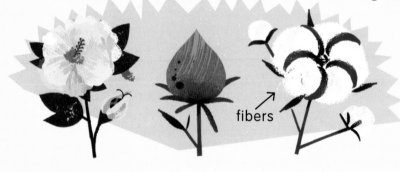

cotton & seeds IN

cotton OUT

seeds OUT

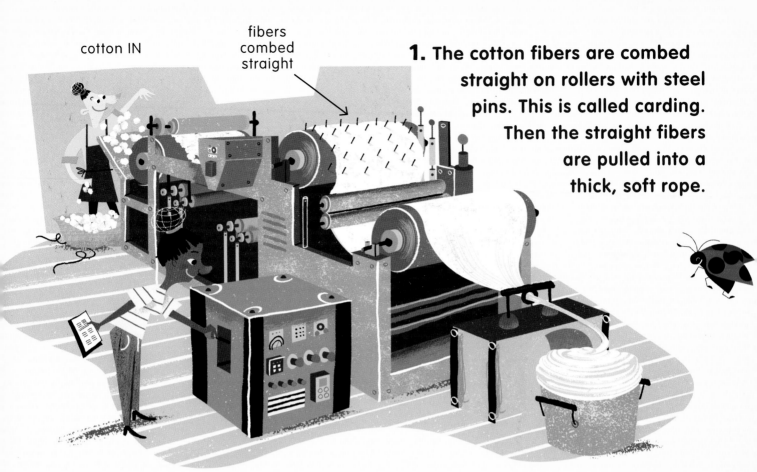

cotton IN

fibers combed straight

1. The cotton fibers are combed straight on rollers with steel pins. This is called carding. Then the straight fibers are pulled into a thick, soft rope.

2. Next a spinning machine stretches the fibers . . . and twists them into a single thread called yarn.

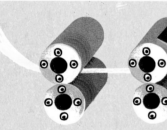
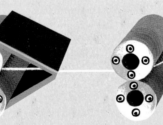

3. In another mill, the yarn is dyed in a bath of purply-blue dye.

Now it's ready to be woven into cloth.

The cotton yarn is woven into cloth on a loom.

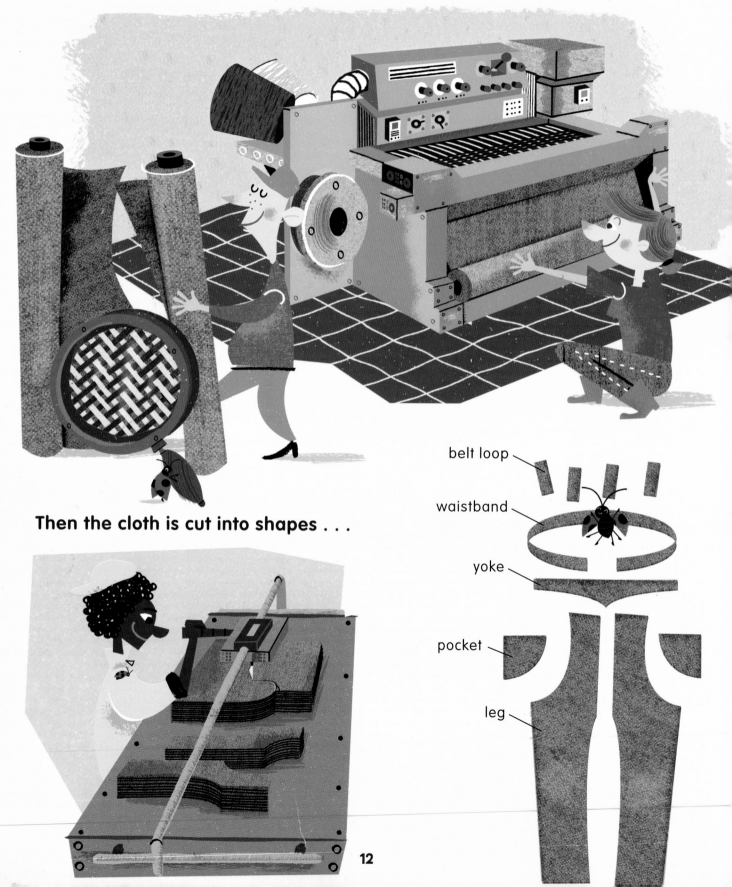

Then the cloth is cut into shapes . . .

belt loop

waistband

yoke

pocket

leg

which are sewn
together into your **JEANS**.

Your jeans are **COOL**
to wear and **STRONG** enough
to stand up to rough stuff.

Clothes are made from
other plants, too.

Linen is
made from
the stalks of flax plants.

It is some of the oldest cloth in the
world. Ancient Egyptians wrapped
their mummies in
it, and the
Romans
wore linen
togas.

The stalks of hemp plants can be
made into cloth, too. It's so strong
that soldiers' uniforms used
to be made of it.

WHAT IS YOUR **SWEATER** MADE OF?

Your sweater is made of wool—the long hair from a sheep. The sheep's wool is c
off once a year (it doesn't hurt the sheep—she's probably glad to be cool again)

Raw wool is dirty and greasy, so it's taken to a mill and washed well.
This is called scouring.

scouring   squeezing   drying

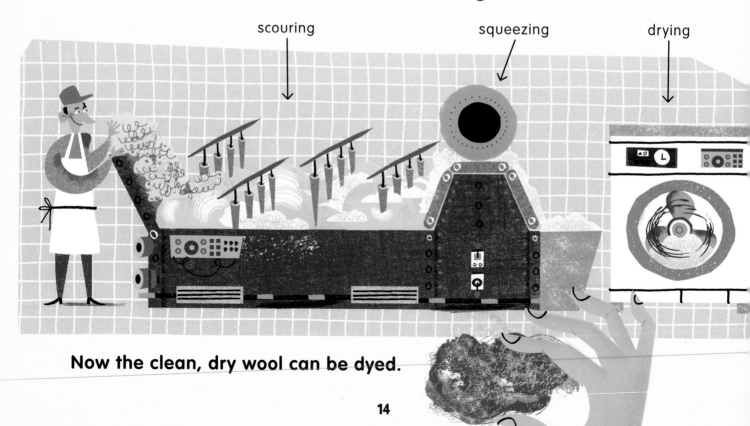

Now the clean, dry wool can be dyed.

A carding machine combs the dry
fibers straight and rolls them into
a thick, soft rope of wool.

Next a spinning machine gently pulls out the stretchy
wool fibers and twists them into yarn.

The yarn is thin, so several strands are twisted together to make wool that is thick enough to knit into clothes.

Knitting can be done on a machine or by hand. Maybe someone in your family knit your sweater!

The wool kept the sheep **WARM**, and now it's a **SWEATER** that's keeping you cozy!

Around the world, people make wool from different long-haired animals.

Yaks in Tibet

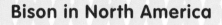

Bison in North America

Camels in China

Llamas and alpacas in South America

Musk oxen in Alaska

Cashmere goats grow extra-soft hair that makes silky, fine sweaters.

The hair from Angora goats is made into soft mohair wool for clothes—and favorite teddy bears!

Angora rabbit wool is REALLY fluffy!

WHAT IS YOUR PARTY DRESS MADE OF?

Some fancy dresses are made of silk.
Silk is the lightest cloth of all, and
it's a fiber made by insects!

Silkworms are not really
worms—they're the
caterpillars of a small
white moth.

Farmers breed thousands of them,
feeding them the leaves
of mulberry trees.

Each silkworm makes a
single silk thread and winds
it into a cocoon around its body.
This single thread can be a mile long!

The cocoons are dried, then softened in hot water.

The super-fine silk threads are gently unrolled and wound around a reel.

These silk threads are pulled and twisted together to make a thicker, stronger yarn.

Then the silk can be dyed bright colors before being woven into cloth on a loom.

Silk can be made into different kinds of cloth: floaty silk, shiny satin, soft taffeta, or rich velvet. In any form, it's ready to be made into your **PARTY DRESS**— perfect for a special occasion.

And YOU feel special when you wear it!

WHAT IS YOUR **SOCCER UNIFORM** MADE O

Your soccer uniform is made of fibers invented by scientists. That's why they're called synthetic or artificial fibers. They have scientific names like polyester and nylon.

1. Synthetic fibers start as a mixture of chemicals that make a kind of sticky syrup.

2. Inside a machine, this syrup is squeezed through tiny holes into thin strands that harden into fibers.

3. The fibers are pulled over rollers and twisted to make a thicker, stronger yarn. Then the yarn is wound onto reels.

Now the yarn is ready to be dyed and woven into cloth.

reel

Cloth made of synthetics is great for **SPORTS CLOTHES**: they **WASH** easily, **DRY** fast, and don't need ironing. (So whoever washes your clothes loves synthetics, too!)

WHAT IS YOUR **FLEECE JACKET** MADE OF?

Don't throw away your plastic bottles: if you recycle them, they can be turned into fleece! It takes about 12 bottles to make your fleece jacket.

At the recycling plant, the plastic is sorted into different colors,

chopped into tiny pieces,

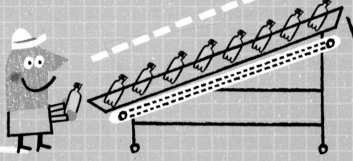

washed . . .

and dried.

1. The pieces are melted into a sticky syrup called polyester.

stretched

2. This syrup is squeezed through tiny holes and comes out as threads that cool and harden.

3. The threads are then stretched out and put through a hot crimping machine, which makes the fibers crinkle.

When they cool, they feel soft and fluffy, like wool.

4. The fibers are carded, spun, and dyed, then knitted into cloth. The cloth is then brushed hard on one side to make it fluff up.

Your **FLEECE JACKET** keeps out chilly winds: zip it up and stay **SNUG!**

WHAT ARE YOUR BOOTS MADE OF?

Rain boots are made from rubber—a juice that comes from a tree!

Rubber trees grow in hot, rainy forests; inside their bark flows a sticky white juice called latex.

Every day workers make a long cut in the bark of each tree (it's called tapping) so the latex runs down and drips into a cup.

The latex is then mixed with acid.

This makes a lumpy mixture that is poured into molds.

It sets and dries into hard blocks.

1. The blocks of rubber are taken to a factory and pushed through hot rollers.

2. This is done over and over again until the rubber is in soft, stretchy sheets.

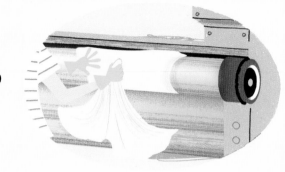

3. As it gets smoother, colors are mixed in.

4. Then the rubber is put through another roller and rolled out into thinner sheets.

5. Boot shapes are cut from the sheets.

6. The shapes are pressed around a boot mold, and their edges are heated to melt them together.

Pull on your **RAIN BOOTS** and stomp in the puddles—your boots are waterproof, so your feet stay **DRY!**

RECYCLING FACTS

Do you have clothes you've grown out of or just don't love anymore?

In the richer parts of the world, people throw away **MILLIONS** of tons of clothes every year.

That's a waste—don't just dump those clothes: **RECYCLE** them!

⊕ Give them to a friend or family member.

⊕ Use the cloth to make useful things like toys, a blanket, or a bag.

⊕ Take them to a thrift shop.

⊕ Turn them into something new—cut down old jeans to make shorts or a skirt!

THRIFT SHOP

AUTHOR'S NOTE

I collect cloth from around the world—I love the colors, the patterns, and how different fabrics feel to the touch. It's amazing to think you can take animal hair or part of a plant, spin it into thread, and then weave, knit, or sew it to make something to wear. Magic!

ILLUSTRATOR'S NOTE

I loved illustrating this book and hope that when children read it, they will realize there's a great story behind everything they wear.

BIBLIOGRAPHY

Gleason, Carrie. **The Biography of Silk.** New York: Crabtree, 2007.

Ridley, Sarah. **A Cotton T-Shirt.** How It's Made series. Milwaukee, WI: Franklin Watts, 2006.

Robson, Deborah, and Carol Ekarius. **The Fleece and Fiber Sourcebook.** North Adams, MA: Storey, 2011.

INDEX

Chris Butterworth is the author of *How Did That Get in My Lunchbox? The Story of Food* and *How Does My Home Work?* She also wrote *Sea Horse: The Shyest Fish in the Sea,* a John Burroughs Nature Books for Young Readers Selection, and many other nonfiction books for young readers. Chris Butterworth lives in Cornwall, England.

Lucia Gaggiotti is the illustrator of *How Did That Get in My Lunchbox? The Story of Food* and *How Does My Home Work?* A graphic designer, packager, and illustrator, she lives in London.